NEVER GIVE UP

summersdale

NEVER GIVE UP

An Hachette UK Company
www.hachette.co.uk

Summersdale Publishers Ltd
Part of Octopus Publishing Group Limited
Carmelite House
50 Victoria Embankment
LONDON
EC4Y 0DZ
UK

www.summersdale.com

Printed and bound in China

ISBN: 978-1-78685-978-5

I'll always
Be with you!
Much Love,

To Seattle Ben

From Sammy

XMAS 2020

Never give up, for that is just the place and time that the tide will turn.

Harriet Beecher Stowe

THROW CAUTION TO THE WIND AND JUST DO IT.

Niamh Greene

Believe in your infinite potential. Your only limitations are those you set upon yourself.

Roy T. Bennett

Owning your story is the bravest thing you will ever do.

Brené Brown

We are what we repeatedly do.

Aristotle

Make the most
of yourself by
fanning the tiny,
inner sparks
of possibility
into flames of
achievement.

Golda Meir

We should not feel embarrassed by our difficulties, only by our failure to grow anything beautiful from them.

Alain de Botton

You're stronger than you believe. Don't let your fear own you.

Michelle Hodkin

You can't be that kid standing at the top of the waterslide, overthinking it. You have to go down the chute.

Tina Fey

The only way of discovering the limits of the possible is to venture a little way past them into the impossible.

Arthur C. Clarke

CHARACTER CONSISTS OF WHAT YOU DO ON THE THIRD AND FOURTH TRIES.

James A. Michener

Dost thou love life? Then do not squander time; for that's the stuff life is made of.

Benjamin Franklin

If my mind can conceive it, if my heart can believe it, I know I can achieve it.

Jesse Jackson

There are no
limits. There are
only plateaus, and
you must not stay
there, you must go
beyond them.

Bruce Lee

Only those who will risk going too far can possibly find out how far one can go.

T. S. Eliot

Find something you're passionate about and keep tremendously interested in it.

Julia Child

THE WAY TO GET STARTED IS TO QUIT TALKING AND BEGIN DOING.

Walt Disney

I have accepted
fear as part of life
– specifically the
fear of change...
I have gone
ahead despite the
pounding in the
heart that says:
turn back.

Erica Jong

Every individual
matters. Every
individual has a
role to play. Every
individual makes
a difference.

Jane Goodall

TRUST YOURSELF. YOU KNOW MORE THAN YOU THINK YOU DO.

Benjamin Spock

Everyone's dream can come true if you just stick to it and work hard.

Serena Williams

Realize that if a door closed, it's because what was behind it wasn't meant for you.

Mandy Hale

I've been absolutely terrified every moment of my life – and I've never let it keep me from doing a single thing I wanted to do.

Georgia O'Keeffe

FORTUNE FAVOURS THE BOLD.

Latin proverb

Do not wait; the time will never be "just right". Start where you stand, and work with whatever tools you may have at your command.

Napoleon Hill

Our greatest glory is not in never falling, but in rising every time we fall.

Oliver Goldsmith

The people who are crazy enough to think that they can change the world are the ones who do.

Steve Jobs

Opportunities don't often come along. So, when they do, you have to grab them.

Audrey Hepburn

The greatest pleasure in life is doing what people say you cannot do.

Walter Bagehot

As one goes through life, one learns that if you don't paddle your own canoe, you don't move.

Katharine Hepburn

In my mind, I've always been an A-list Hollywood superstar. Y'all just didn't know yet.

Will Smith

Stop wearing your wishbone where your backbone ought to be.

Elizabeth Gilbert

It is good to have
an end to journey
toward; but it is
the journey that
matters, in the end.

Ursula K. Le Guin

EVER TRIED.
EVER FAILED.
NO MATTER.
TRY AGAIN.
FAIL AGAIN.
FAIL BETTER.

Samuel Beckett

Stay afraid, but do it anyway. What's important is the action. You don't have to wait to be confident.

Carrie Fisher

Courage calls to courage everywhere, and its voice cannot be denied.

Millicent Fawcett

Doubt kills more dreams than failure ever will.

Suzy Kassem

If we are not
willing to fail
we will never
accomplish anything.
All creative acts
involve the risk
of failure.

Madeleine L'Engle

I am learning every day to allow the space between where I am and where I want to be to inspire me and not terrify me.

Tracee Ellis Ross

Leap, and
the net will
appear.

Anonymous

Think like a queen. A queen is not afraid to fail. Failure is another stepping stone to greatness.

Oprah Winfrey

Know the wolves that hunt you. In time, they will be the dogs that bring your slippers.

Kate Tempest

NOTHING WILL WORK UNLESS YOU DO.

Maya Angelou

You've got to make choices that make sense for you, because there's always going to be somebody who'll think you should do something differently.

Michelle Obama

You must
find the place
within yourself
where nothing
is impossible.

Deepak Chopra

Sometimes you can do everything right and things will still go wrong. The key is to never stop doing right.

Angie Thomas

If you had started doing anything two weeks ago, by today you would have been two weeks better at it.

John Mayer

The most effective way to do it is to do it.

Amelia Earhart

THERE ARE NO SHORTCUTS TO ANY PLACE WORTH GOING.

Beverly Sills

Courage doesn't always roar. Sometimes courage is the quiet voice at the end of the day saying, "I will try again tomorrow."

Mary Anne Radmacher

Fear of making mistakes can itself become a huge mistake... for life is risky and anything less is already a loss.

Rebecca Solnit

BE YOURSELF. THE WORLD WORSHIPS THE ORIGINAL.

Ingrid Bergman

**Somewhere,
something
incredible
is waiting to
be known.**

Sharon Begley

If you were born without wings, do nothing to prevent them from growing.

Coco Chanel

Keep your eyes on
the stars, but
remember to keep
your feet on
the ground.

Theodore Roosevelt

IMPOSSIBLE IS NOTHING.

Boyd Coyner

The future rewards those who press on. I don't have time to feel sorry for myself. I don't have time to complain. I'm going to press on.

Barack Obama

You can,
you should,
and if you're
brave enough
to start,
you will.

Stephen King

Who seeks shall find.

Sophocles

Stop letting people who do so little for you control so much of your mind, feelings and emotions.

Will Smith

Any transition is easier if you believe in yourself and your talent.

Priyanka Chopra

Success is a state of mind. If you want success, start thinking of yourself as a success.

Joyce Brothers

I care not so
much what I am
to others as what
I am to myself.

Michel de Montaigne

Knowing what must be done does away with fear.

Rosa Parks

Real difficulties can be overcome. It is only the imaginary ones that are unconquerable.

Theodore N. Vail

LIMIT YOUR "ALWAYS" AND YOUR "NEVERS".

Amy Poehler

You are enough,
just as you are,
just as you were
made to be.

Melissa Camara Wilkins

**Let us make
our future now,
and let us make
our dreams
tomorrow's reality.**

Malala Yousafzai

It's not who you are that holds you back; it's who you think you're not.

Eric Thomas

It is the same with people as it is with riding a bike. Only when moving can one comfortably maintain one's balance.

Albert Einstein

We can push ourselves further. We always have more to give.

Simone Biles

Don't raise your voice; improve your argument.

Desmond Tutu

If you want light
to come into your
life, you need
to stand where
it is shining.

Guy Finley

Surround yourself with those who only lift you higher.

Oprah Winfrey

I AM THE GREATEST. I SAID THAT EVEN BEFORE I KNEW I WAS.

Muhammad Ali

It never will rain
roses: when we want
To have more roses
we must plant
more trees.

George Eliot

Don't wait to be sure. Move, move, move.

Miranda July

Whatever the present moment contains, accept it as if you had chosen it. Always work with it, not against it.

Eckhart Tolle

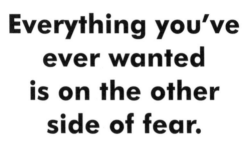

Everything you've ever wanted is on the other side of fear.

George Addair

The best preparation for tomorrow is doing your best today.

H. Jackson Brown Jr

EITHER YOU RUN THE DAY OR THE DAY RUNS YOU.

Jim Rohn

Nothing is a mistake. There's no win and no fail. There's only make.

Corita Kent

When you're knocked
down, get right
back up and never
listen to anyone
who says you can't
or shouldn't go on.

Hillary Clinton

OUT OF DIFFICULTIES GROW MIRACLES.

Jean de La Bruyère

You can do anything you want, even if you are being told negative things. Stay strong and find motivation.

Misty Copeland

Identify your problems, but give your power and energy to solutions.

Tony Robbins

Don't ever doubt
yourselves or waste
a second of your
life. It's too
short, and you're
too special.

Ariana Grande

OPPORTUNITIES DON'T HAPPEN; YOU CREATE THEM.

Chris Grosser

Never forget what you are... Make it your strength... Armour yourself in it, and it will never be used to hurt you.

George R. R. Martin

We must not
allow other
people's
limited
perceptions
to define us.

Virginia Satir

The bamboo that bends is stronger than the oak that resists.

Japanese proverb

To accomplish great things, we must not only act, but also dream; not only plan, but also believe.

Anatole France

The choice to have a great attitude is something that nobody or no circumstance can take away from you.

Zig Ziglar

There are
plenty of difficult
obstacles in your
path. Don't allow
yourself to become
one of them.

Ralph Marston

The man who moves
a mountain begins
by carrying away
small stones.

Confucius

Look up, laugh loud, talk big, keep the colour in your cheek and the fire in your eye.

William Hazlitt

I didn't get there
by wishing for it or
hoping for it, but by
working for it.

Estée Lauder

EVERY ARTIST WAS FIRST AN AMATEUR.

Ralph Waldo Emerson

There is always
a realistic way to
fulfil any dream.
There has never
been a dream that
you can't have.

Barbara Sher

It is hard to fail,
but it is worse
never to have
tried to succeed.

Theodore Roosevelt

There is no one giant step that does it. It's a lot of little steps.

Peter A. Cohen

There will be
obstacles. There
will be doubters.
There will be
mistakes. But with
hard work… there
are no limits.

Michael Phelps

Never bend your head; always hold it high; look the world straight in the eye.

Helen Keller

Be brave.
Take risks.
Nothing can
substitute
experience.

Paulo Coelho

True stories seldom have endings. I don't want a happy ending; I want more story.

Frances Hardinge

Often when you think you're at the end of something, you're at the beginning of something else.

Fred Rogers

OPTIMISM CAN BE RELEARNT.

Marian Keyes

There is nothing in
a caterpillar that
tells you it's going
to be a butterfly.

Buckminster Fuller

A step
backward,
after making
a wrong turn,
is a step in the
right direction.

Kurt Vonnegut

When you learn from your mistakes, then you stop caring about what people who don't know you think.

Beyoncé

The doing is the thing. The talking and worrying and thinking is not the thing.

Amy Poehler

Believe in yourself and you can achieve greatness in your life.

Judy Blume

YOU DEFEAT DEFEATISM WITH CONFIDENCE.

Vince Lombardi

Scared is what
you're feeling...
brave is what
you're doing.

Emma Donoghue

Just don't
give up trying
to do what you
really want to do.
Where there is love
and inspiration,
I don't think you
can go wrong.

Ella Fitzgerald

I DWELL IN POSSIBILITY.

Emily Dickinson

You have just one life to live. It is yours. Own it, claim it, live it, do the best you can with it.

Hillary Clinton

So whatever
you want to
do, just do it...
Making a damn
fool of yourself
is absolutely
essential.

Gloria Steinem

You've got to get up every morning with determination if you're going to go to bed with satisfaction.

George Lorimer

IF IT DOESN'T SCARE YOU, YOU'RE PROBABLY NOT DREAMING BIG ENOUGH.

Tory Burch

What separates the talented individual from the successful one is a lot of hard work.

Stephen King

Dream lofty dreams, and as you dream, so shall you become.

James Allen

Go confidently in the direction of your dreams. Live the life you have imagined.

Henry David Thoreau

Life is ten per cent what happens to me and ninety per cent how I react to it.

Charles Swindoll

It's not what we do once in a while that shapes our lives, but what we do consistently.

Tony Robbins

Believe that life is worth living and your belief will help create the fact.

William James

What you can do,
or dream you can,
begin it. Boldness
has genius, power
and magic in it.

John Anster

If you can find a path with no obstacles, it probably doesn't lead anywhere.

Anonymous

Don't ask what the world needs. Ask what makes you come alive and go do it.

Howard Thurman

JUST BREATHE AND BELIEVE.

Jodi Livon

With persistence
a drop of water
hollows out
the stone.

Choerilus of Samos

Don't judge each day by the harvest you reap, but by the seeds you plant.

Anonymous

Consider everything an experiment.

Corita Kent

All of my life,
I've jumped off the
cliff and built
my wings. It works
every single time.

Ray Bradbury

IT'S NOT THE MOUNTAINS WE CONQUER, BUT OURSELVES.

Edmund Hillary

If you
really want
something,
you can figure
out how
to make it
happen.

Cher

You are never too old to set another goal or to dream a new dream.

Les Brown

Don't you ever let a soul in the world tell you that you can't be exactly who you are.

Lady Gaga

SPEAK UP. BELIEVE IN YOURSELF. TAKE RISKS.

Sheryl Sandberg

The world doesn't care how many times you fall down, as long as it's one fewer than the number of times you get back up.

Aaron Sorkin

One can
never consent
to creep when
one feels an
impulse
to soar.

Helen Keller

I was very passionate about what I did and I never gave up. That's why everything happened the way it did in my career.

Michael Phelps

I really think
a champion is
defined not by
their wins but
by how they can
recover when
they fall.

Serena Williams

The only person I really believe in is me.

Debbie Harry

I SHALL EITHER FIND A WAY OR MAKE ONE.

Hannibal Barca

The most common way people give up their power is by thinking they don't have any.

Alice Walker

I've learned
throughout my
journey that
perfection is the
enemy of greatness.

Janelle Monáe

I AM NOT A HAS-BEEN. I AM A WILL BE.

Lauren Bacall

I try to not have anything I do be dictated by what others expect.

Samantha Ronson

If they don't give you a seat at the table, bring a folding chair.

Shirley Chisholm

Never abandon your dreams. You may regret it for the rest of your life.

Fabiola Gianotti

WE CAN ENDURE MUCH MORE THAN WE THINK WE CAN.

Frida Kahlo

Showing up fully exactly where you are is the fastest way to get where you want to go.

Marie Forleo

Life changes very quickly, in a very positive way, if you let it.

Lindsey Vonn

The man who really counts in the world is the doer... not the man who only talks or writes about how it ought to be done.

Theodore Roosevelt

Survival can be summed up in three words – never give up. That's the heart of it really. Just keep trying.

Bear Grylls

If you're interested in finding out more about our books, find us on Facebook at **Summersdale Publishers** and follow us on Twitter at @Summersdale.

www.summersdale.com